Handbook of Tigers

Editor

Nelly Deaton

Scribbles

Year of Publication 2018

ISBN : 9789352979783

Book Published by

Scribbles

(An Imprint of Alpha Editions)

email - alphaedis@gmail.com

Produced by: PediaPress GmbH
Limburg an der Lahn
Germany
http://pediapress.com/

The content within this book was generated collaboratively by volunteers. Please be advised that nothing found here has necessarily been reviewed by people with the expertise required to provide you with complete, accurate or reliable information. Some information in this book may be misleading or simply wrong. Alpha Editions and PediaPress does not guarantee the validity of the information found here. If you need specific advice (for example, medical, legal, financial, or risk management) please seek a professional who is licensed or knowledgeable in that area.

Sources, licenses and contributors of the articles and images are listed in the section entitled "References". Parts of the books may be licensed under the GNU Free Documentation License. A copy of this license is included in the section entitled "GNU Free Documentation License"

The views and characters expressed in the book are those of the contributors and his/her imagination and do not represent the views of the Publisher.

Contents

Tiger

Tiger
Temporal range: early Pleistocene–Present PreЄ€ OSD C P T J K PgN
A Bengal tiger (*P. t. tigris*) at Kanha National Park, India
Conservation status
 Endangered (IUCN 3.1)

Scientific classification 🖉	
Kingdom:	Animalia
Phylum:	Chordata
Class:	Mammalia
Order:	Carnivora
Suborder:	Feliformia
Family:	Felidae
Subfamily:	Pantherinae
Genus:	*Panthera*
Species:	***P. tigris***

Binomial name
Panthera tigris (Linnaeus, 1758)
Subspecies

P. t. tigris
P. t. sondaica

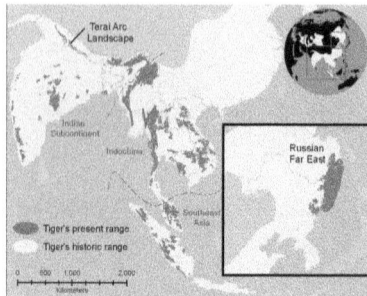

Tiger's historic range in about 1850 (pale yellow) and in 2006 (in green).

Synonyms

- *Felis tigris* Linnaeus, 1758
- *Tigris striatus* Severtzov, 1858
- *Tigris regalis* Gray, 1867

The **tiger** (*Panthera tigris*) is the largest cat species, most recognizable for its pattern of dark vertical stripes on reddish-orange fur with a lighter underside. The species is classified in the genus *Panthera* with the lion, leopard, jaguar and snow leopard. It is an apex predator, primarily preying on ungulates such as deer and bovids. It is territorial and generally a solitary but social predator, often requiring large contiguous areas of habitat that support its prey requirements. This, coupled with the fact that it is indigenous to some of the more densely populated places on Earth, has caused significant conflicts with humans.

The tiger is among the most recognisable and popular of the world's charismatic megafauna. It featured prominently in ancient mythology and folklore and continues to be depicted in modern films and literature, appearing on many flags, coats of arms and as mascots for sporting teams. The tiger is the national animal of India, Bangladesh, Malaysia and South Korea.

Etymology

The Middle English *tigre* and Old English *tigras* (plural) derive from Old French *tigre*, from Latin *tigris*. This was a borrowing of Classical Greek τίγρις (transliterated as *tigris*, the modern species name), a foreign borrowing of unknown orgin meaning "tiger" as well as the river Tigris. The original source may have been Persian *tigra* (pointed or sharp), and Avestan *tigrhi* (arrow),

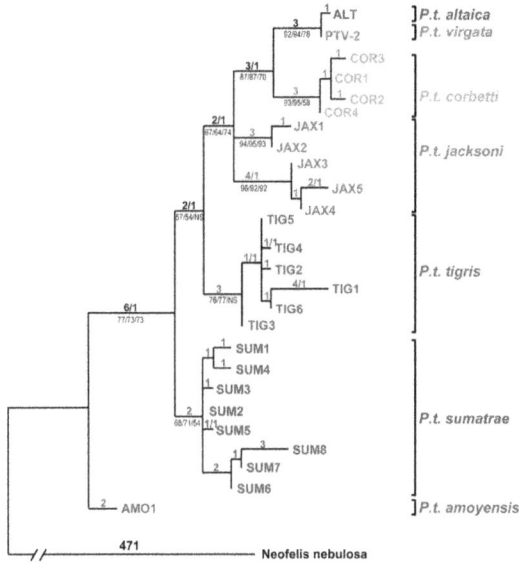

Figure 1: *Tiger phylogenetic relationships*

perhaps referring to the speed of the tiger's leap, although these words are not known to have any meanings associated with tigers.[1]

The genus name *Panthera* is traceable to Old French *pantère*, from Latin *panthera*, from Ancient Greek *panther*, most likely with the original meaning "yellowish animal", or from *pandarah* meaning "whitish-yellow", possibly related to Sanskrit *pundarikas* (tiger).[2] The derivation from Greek *pan-* ("all") and *ther* ("beast") is likely incorrect folk etymology.[3]

Taxonomy and genetics

In 1758, Carl Linnaeus described the tiger in his work *Systema Naturae* and gave it the scientific name *Felis tigris*. In 1929, the British taxonomist Reginald Innes Pocock subordinated the species under the genus *Panthera* using the scientific name *Panthera tigris*.

Evolution

The tiger's closest living relatives were previously thought to be the *Panthera* species lion, leopard and jaguar. Results of genetic analysis indicate that about 2.88 million years ago, the tiger and the snow leopard lineages diverged from the other *Panthera* species, and that both may be more closely related to each

Figure 2: *Restoration of Panthera zdanskyi, an extinct relative whose oldest remains were found in northwest China, suggesting the origins of the tiger lineage*

other than to the lion, leopard and jaguar. Results of a phylogeographic study indicate that all living tigers had a common ancestor 72,000–108,000 years ago.

Fossil remains of the Longdan tiger were found in the Gansu province of north-western China. This species lived at the beginning of the Pleistocene, about 2 million years ago, and is considered to be a sister taxon of the modern tiger. It was about the size of a jaguar and probably had a different coat pattern. Despite being considered more "primitive", the Longdan tiger was functionally and possibly ecologically similar to the modern tiger. As it lived in north-western China, that may have been where the tiger lineage originated. Tigers grew in size, possibly in response to adaptive radiations of prey species like deer and bovids, which may have occurred in Southeast Asia during the early Pleistocene.

The earliest fossils of true tigers are known from the early and middle Pleistocene deposits in China and Sumatra, around 2 million years ago. The Trinil tiger (*Panthera tigris trinilensis*) lived about 1.2 million years ago and is known from fossils found at Trinil in Java. The Wanhsien, Ngandong, Trinil and Japanese tigers became extinct in prehistoric times. Tigers first reached India and northern Asia in the late Pleistocene, reaching eastern Beringia, Japan, and Sakhalin. Some fossil skulls are morphologically distinct from lion skulls, which could indicate tiger presence in Alaska during the last glacial period, about 100,000 years ago. Fossils found in Japan indicate the local tigers were smaller than the mainland forms, possibly due to insular dwarfism.

The tiger's full genome sequence was published in 2013. It was found to have similar repeat composition than other cat genomes and an appreciably conserved synteny.

Recent subspecies

Following Linnaeus's first descriptions of the species, several tiger specimens were described and proposed as subspecies. The validity of several tiger subspecies was questioned in 1999. Most putative subspecies described in the 19th and 20th centuries were distinguished on basis of fur length and coloration, striping patterns and body size, hence characteristics that vary widely within populations. Morphologically, tigers from different regions vary little, and gene flow between populations in those regions is considered to have been possible during the Pleistocene. Therefore, it was proposed to recognize only two tiger subspecies as valid, namely *P. t. tigris* in mainland Asia, and *P. t. sondaica* in the Greater Sunda Islands and possibly in Sundaland.

Results of craniological analysis of 111 tiger skulls from Southeast Asian range countries indicate that Sumatran tiger skulls differ from Indochinese and Javan tiger skulls, whereas Bali tiger skulls are similar in size to Javan tiger skulls. The authors proposed to classify Sumatran and Javan tiger as distinct species, *P. sumatrae* and *P. sondaica* with Bali tiger as subspecies *P. sondaica balica*.

In 2015, morphological, ecological and molecular traits of all putative tiger subspecies were analysed in a combined approach. Results support distinction of the two evolutionary groups continental and Sunda tigers. The authors proposed recognition of only two subspecies, namely *P. t. tigris* comprising the Bengal, Malayan, Indochinese, South Chinese, Siberian and Caspian tiger populations, and *P. t. sondaica* comprising the Javan, Bali and Sumatran tiger populations. The authors also noted that this reclassification will affect tiger conservation management. One conservation specialist welcomed this proposal as it would make captive breeding programmes and future rewilding of zoo-born tigers easier. One geneticist was sceptical of this study and maintained that the currently recognised nine subspecies can be distinguished genetically.

In 2017, the Cat Classification Task Force of the IUCN Cat Specialist Group revised felid taxonomy and now recognizes the tiger populations in continental Asia as *P. t. tigris*, and those in the Sunda Islands as *P. t. sondaica*.

The following table is based on the classification of the species *Panthera tigris* provided in *Mammal Species of the World*. It also reflects the classification used by the Cat Classification Task Force:

Non-insular Asia

Subspecies	Description	Image
Bengal tiger (*P. t. tigris*) (Linnaeus, 1758)	The Bengal tiger's coat colour varies from light yellow to reddish yellow with black stripes. Males attain a total nose-to-tail length of 270 to 310 cm (110 to 120 in) and weigh between 180 to 258 kg (397 to 569 lb), while females range from 240 to 265 cm (94 to 104 in) and 100 to 160 kg (220 to 350 lb).[4] In northern India and Nepal, the average is larger; males weigh up to 235 kilograms (518 lb), while females average 140 kilograms (310 lb). Recorded body weights of wild individuals indicate that it is the heaviest subspecies.[5] This population occurs in Bangladesh, Bhutan, India, Nepal, foremost in alluvial grasslands, subtropical and tropical rainforests, scrub forests, wet and dry deciduous forests and mangrove habitats. It is extinct in Pakistan. In 2014, the population in India was estimated at 2,226 mature individuals, 163–253 in Nepal and 103 in Bhutan.	
Caspian tiger (*P. t. tigris*), formerly *P. t. virgata* (Illiger, 1815)	The Caspian tiger was described as having narrow and closely set stripes. The size of its skull did not differ significantly from that of the Bengal tiger. According to genetic analysis, it was closely related to the Siberian tiger. The population inhabited forests and riverine corridors from Eastern Anatolia, South Caucasus and coast of Caspian Sea, along the coast of the Aral Sea, in Amu-Darya and Syr-Darya basins to the southern shore of Lake Balkhash and into the Altai Mountains. It had been recorded in the wild until the early 1970s and is considered extinct since the late 20th century.	
Siberian tiger (*P. t. tigris*), formerly *P. t. altaica* (Temminck, 1844). Also known as the Amur tiger.	The Siberian tiger is the world's largest extant tiger in captivity. It has a thick coat with pale hues and few dark brown stripes. Males have a head and body length of between 190 and 230 cm (75 and 91 in) and weigh between 180 and 306 kg (397 and 675 lb), while females average 160 to 180 cm (63 to 71 in) and 100 to 167 kg (220 to 368 lb). Tail length is about 60–110 cm (24–43 in). This population inhabits the Amur-Ussuri region of Primorsky Krai and Khabarovsk Krai in far eastern Siberia, with a small population in Hunchun National Siberian Tiger Nature Reserve in northeastern China near the border to North Korea. It is extinct in Mongolia, North Korea, and South Korea. In 2005, there were 331–393 adult and subadult Siberian tigers in the region, with a breeding adult population of about 250 individuals. As of 2015, there was an estimated population of 480-540 individuals in the Russian Far East.	

Indochinese tiger (*P. t. tigris*), formerly *P. t. corbetti* Mazák, 1968	The Indochinese tiger was described as being smaller than the Bengal tiger and as having a smaller skull. Males average 108 inches (270 cm) in total length and weigh between 150 and 195 kg (331 and 430 lb), while females average 96 inches (240 cm) and 100–130 kg (220–290 lb). This population occurs in Myanmar, Thailand, Laos, but has not been recorded in Vietnam since 1997. In 2010, the population in Indochina was estimated at about 350 individuals. In Southeast Asia, tiger populations have declined in key areas and are threatened by illegal production of tiger bone for use in traditional medicine.	
Malayan tiger (*P. t. tigris*), formerly *P. t. jacksoni* Luo et al., 2004	There is no clear difference between the Malayan and the Indochinese tiger in pelage or skull size. It was proposed as a distinct subspecies on the basis of mtDNA and microsatellite sequences that differs from the Indochinese tiger. Males range in total length from 190–280 cm (75–110 in) and weigh between 47.2 to 129.1 kg (104 to 285 lb), while females range from 180–260 cm (71–102 in) and 24 to 88 kg (53 to 194 lb). The population was roughly estimated at 250 to 340 adult individuals in 2013, and likely comprised less than 200 mature breeding individuals at the time. The geographic division between Malayan and Indochinese tigers is unclear as tiger populations in northern Malaysia are contiguous with those in southern Thailand. In Singapore the last tiger was shot in 1932; tigers are considered extirpated since the 1950s.	
South China tiger (*P. t. tigris*), formerly *P. t. amoyensis* (Hilzheimer, 1905)	The South China tiger is considered to be the most ancient of the tiger subspecies and is distinguished by a particularly narrow skull, long-muzzled nose, rhombus-like stripes and vivid orange colour. Males range in total length from 230–260 cm (91–102 in) and weigh between 130 to 180 kg (290 to 400 lb), while females range from 220–240 cm (87–94 in) and 100 to 110 kg (220 to 240 lb). Aside from the fact that it was grouped with other mainland populations under *P. t. tigris*, it was noted to have unique mtDNA. The population is extinct in the wild. Despite unconfirmed reports and some evidence of footprints, there has been no confirmed sighting in China since the early 1970s. As of 2007, the captive population consisted of 73 individuals, which derived from six wild founders.	

Sunda Islands

Subspecies	Description	Image
Javan tiger (*P. t. sondaica*) (Temminck, 1844)	The Javan tiger was small compared to tigers of the Asian mainland. Males weighed 100–141 kg (220–311 lb) and females 75–115 kg (165–254 lb). This population was limited to the Indonesian island of Java, and had been recorded until the mid-1970s. After 1979, no more sightings were confirmed in the region of Mount Betiri. An expedition to Mount Halimun Salak National Park in 1990 did not yield any definite, direct evidence for the continued existence of tigers.	

Bali tiger (*P. t. sondaica*), formerly *P. t. balica* (Schwarz, 1912)	The Bali tiger was the smallest tiger and limited to the Indonesian island of Bali. It had a weight of 90–100 kg (200–220 lb) in males and 65–80 kg (143–176 lb) in females. A typical feature of Bali tiger skulls is the narrow occipital plane, which is analogous with the shape of skulls of Javan tigers. In Bali, tigers were hunted to extinction; the last Bali tiger, an adult female, is thought to have been killed at Sumbar Kima, West Bali, on 27 September 1937, though there were unconfirmed reports that villagers found a tiger corpse in 1963.	
Sumatran tiger (*P. t. sondaica*), formerly *P. t. sumatrae* Pocock, 1929	It is the smallest of all living tigers. Males range in total length from 220 to 255 cm (87 to 100 in) and weigh between 100 to 140 kg (220 to 310 lb), while females range between 215 to 230 cm (85 to 91 in) and 75 to 110 kg (165 to 243 lb). The reasons for its small size compared to mainland tigers are unclear, but probably the result of competition for limited and small prey. The population is thought to be of Asia mainland origin and to have been isolated about 6,000 to 12,000 years ago after a rise in sea-level created the Indonesian island of Sumatra. The population is the last surviving of the three Indonesian island tiger populations. It is listed as Critically Endangered on the IUCN Red List. By 2008, the wild population was estimated at between 441 and 679 in 10 protected areas covering about 52,000 km^2 (20,000 sq mi).	

Hybrids

Lions have been known to breed with tigers in captivity to create hybrids called ligers and tigons. They share physical and behavioural qualities of both parent species. Such hybrids were once commonly bred in zoos, but this is now discouraged due to the emphasis on conservation. The liger is a cross between a male lion and a tigress. Ligers are typically between 10 and 12 ft (3.0 and 3.7 m) in length, and can weigh between 800 and 1,000 lb (360 and 450 kg) or more. Because the lion sire passes on a growth-promoting gene, but the corresponding growth-inhibiting gene from the female tiger is absent, ligers grow far larger than either parent species.

The less common tigon is a cross between a lioness and a male tiger. Because the male tiger does not pass on a growth-promoting gene and the lioness passes on a growth inhibiting gene, tigons are around the same size as their parents. Females are sometimes fertile and have occasionally given birth to litigons when mated to a male Asiatic lion.

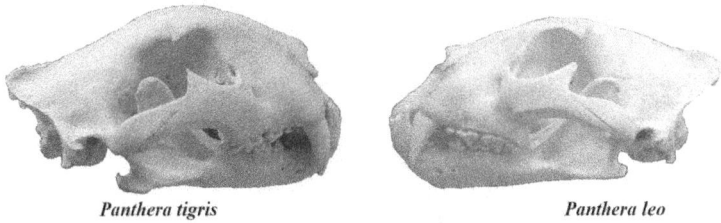

Panthera tigris   *Panthera leo*

Figure 3: *Though the tiger's skull is similar to that of the lion,*
the lower jaw structure is a reliable indicator of the species

Characteristics

The tiger has a muscular body with powerful forelimbs, a large head and a
tail that is about half the length of its body. Its pelage is dense and heavy,
and colouration varies between shades of orange and brown with white ventral
areas and distinctive vertical black stripes that are unique in each individual.
Stripes are likely advantageous for camouflage in vegetation such as long grass
with strong vertical patterns of light and shade. The tiger is one of only a few
striped cat species; it is not known why spotted patterns and rosettes are the
more common camouflage pattern among felids. A tiger's coat pattern is still
visible when it is shaved. This is not due to skin pigmentation, but to the stub-
ble and hair follicles embedded in the skin, similar to human beards (colloqui-
ally five o'clock shadow), and is in common with other big cats. They have a
mane-like heavy growth of fur around the neck and jaws and long whiskers,
especially in males. The pupils are circular with yellow irises. The small,
rounded ears have a prominent white spot on the back, surrounded by black.
These false "eyespots", called ocelli, apparently play an important role in in-
traspecies communication.

The tiger's skull is similar to a lion's skull, with the frontal region usually less
depressed or flattened, and a slightly longer postorbital region. The lion skull
shows broader nasal openings. Due to the variation in skull sizes of the two
species, the structure of the lower jaw is a reliable indicator for their identi-
fcation. The tiger has fairly stout teeth; its somewhat curved canines are the
longest among living felids with a crown height of up to 90 mm (3.5 in).

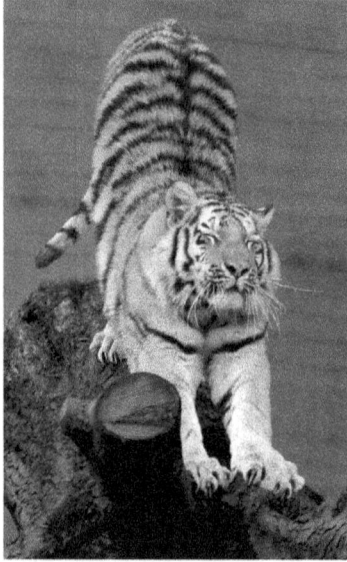

Figure 4: *Siberian tiger, the largest tiger in captivity, but not in the wild, and the tallest tiger at the shoulder, besides the Bengal tiger*

Size

Tigers are the most variable in size of all big cat species. There is a notable sexual dimorphism between males and females, with the latter being consistently smaller than males. The size difference between males and females is proportionally greater in the large tiger subspecies, with males weighing up to 1.7 times more than females. Males also have wider forepaw pads than females, enabling gender to be told from tracks.

Generally, males vary in total length from 250 to 390 cm (8.2 to 12.8 ft) and weigh between 90 to 306 kg (198 to 675 lb) with skull length ranging from 316 to 383 mm (12.4 to 15.1 in). Females vary in total length from 200 to 275 cm (6.56 to 9.02 ft), weigh 65 to 167 kg (143 to 368 lb) with skull length ranging from 268 to 318 mm (0.879 to 1.043 ft). The heaviest wild tiger ever reported had a total body length of 3.38 m (11.1 ft) over curves. In either sex, the tail represents about 0.6 to 1.1 m (24 to 43 in) of total length.

Large male Siberian tigers reach a total length of more than 3.5 m (11.5 ft) over curves and 3.3 m (10.8 ft) between the pegs, with a weight of up to at least 300 kg (660 lb). This is considerably larger than the weight of 75 to 140 kg (165 to 309 lb) reached by the Sumatran tiger. At the shoulder, tigers may variously stand 0.7 to 1.22 m (2.3 to 4.0 ft) tall. The heaviest captive

Figure 5: *White tigers, this recessive colour variant is found in the Bengal tigers, and with regular stripes and blue eyes. It is not albinism*

tiger was a Siberian tiger at 465 kg (1,025 lb). It has been hypothesised that body size of different tiger populations may be correlated with climate and be explained by thermoregulation and Bergmann's rule, or by distribution and size of available prey species. However, the heaviest wild tiger on record was a Bengal tiger from north India which was shot in 1967. It allegedly weighed 388.7 kg (857 lb), though it should be noted that it had a heavy meal before it was killedwithout which it would have weighed significantly less. Likewise, the record length for a tiger's skull was 16.25 in (413 mm) "over the bone" for a tiger that was shot in 1927 in northern India.

The Bengal and Siberian tigers are amongst the tallest cats in shoulder height. They are also ranked with the Caspian tiger among the biggest cats that ever existed. However, on average, a wild adult male Siberian tiger at 176.4 kilograms (389 lb) body weight is outweighed by an adult, male Bengal tiger at 196 kilograms (432 lb).

Colour variations

A well-known allele found only in the Bengal population produces the white tiger, a colour variant first recorded in the Mughal Empire in the late 16th and early 17th centuries. Genetically, whiteness is recessive: a cub is white only

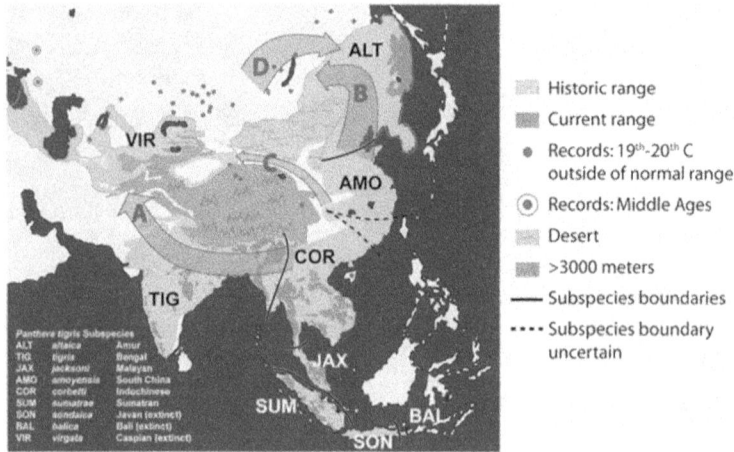

Figure 6: *Historical distribution*

when both parents carry the allele for whiteness. It is not albinism, pigment being evident in the white tiger's stripes and in their blue eyes. The causative mutation changes a single amino acid in the transporter protein SLC45A2. White tigers are more frequently bred in captivity, where the comparatively small gene pool can lead to inbreeding. This has given white tigers a greater likelihood of being born with physical defects, such as cleft palate, scoliosis (curvature of the spine), and strabismus (squint).

True albino tigers do exist and may be termed "snow white" tigers. In this colour morph, the stripes are extremely faint on the body while the tail has pale reddish-brown rings. Golden tigers, another colour morph, have pale golden pelage with a blond tone and reddish-brown stripes. These types are rarely recorded in the wild. Both snow white and golden tiger are homozygous for the *CORIN* gene.

Distribution and habitat

Tiger populations once ranged widely across Asia, from the Black Sea in the west to Kolyma and Sumatra in the east and to the Indian Ocean in the south. Over the past 100 years, the species has lost 93% of its historic range and has been extirpated from Western and Central Asia, the islands of Java and Bali and large areas of Southeast, South and East Asia. Today, its ecological habitats include the Siberian taiga as well as open grasslands and tropical mangrove swamps, and it has been classified as endangered in the IUCN Red List. Major reasons for the population decline include habitat destruction, habitat fragmentation and poaching. The extent of area inhabited by tigers is estimated at less than 1,184,911 km^2 (457,497 sq mi), a 41% decline from that of the mid-1990s. The global wild population is estimated to number between 3,062 and 3,948 individuals, down from around 100,000 at the start of the 20th century, with most remaining populations occurring in small pockets isolated from each other and with 2,000 of the total population living on the Indian subcontinent. In 2016, an estimate of a global wild tiger population of approximately 3,890 individuals was presented during the Third Asia Ministerial Conference on Tiger Conservation. The WWF subsequently declared that the world's count of wild tigers had risen for the first time in a century.

At the end of the last glacial period about 20,000 years ago, the tiger was widespread from Eastern Anatolia Region and Mesopotamia, in Central Asia to eastern Siberia and South and Southeast Asia to the Indonesian islands of Java, Bali and Sumatra. Today, tigers are regionally extinct in Afghanistan, Ukraine, Kazakhstan, Kyrgyzstan, Tajikistan, Turkmenistan, Iran, Pakistan and Singapore.

Fossil remains of tigers were excavated in Sri Lanka, China, Japan, Sarawak and the Philippine island of Palawan dating to the late Pliocene, Pleistocene and Early Holocene. The Bornean tiger was apparently present in Borneo between the Late Pleistocene to the Holocene, but may have gone extinct in prehistoric times.

During the 20th century, tigers became extinct in Western and Central Asia, and in a number of Sunda Islands, and were restricted to isolated pockets in the remaining parts of their range. They were extirpated on the island of Bali in the 1940s, around the Caspian Sea in the 1970s, and on Java in the 1980s. This was the result of habitat loss and the ongoing killing of tigers and tiger prey. Today, their significantly fragmented and depopulated range extends eastward from India to Bangladesh, Bhutan, Nepal, Myanmar, Thailand, Cambodia, Laos, Vietnam, China, Malaysia, Indonesia, North Korea and Russia. The northern limit of their range is close to the Amur River in southeastern Siberia. The only large island they still inhabit is Sumatra. Since the beginning of the 20th century, tigers' historical range has shrunk by 93%. In the decade from 1997 to 2007, the estimated area known to be occupied by tigers has declined by 41%.[6]

The tiger occupies a wide range of habitat types, but will usually require sufficient cover, proximity to water, and an abundance of prey. It prefers dense vegetation, for which its camouflage colouring is ideally suited, and where a single predator is not at a disadvantage compared with the multiple cats in a pride. A further habitat requirement is the placement of suitably secluded

Figure 7: *Tigers are comfortable in water and frequently bathe*

den locations, which may consist of caves, large hollow trees, or dense vegetation. The Bengal tiger in particular lives in many types of forests, including
wet, evergreen, and the semi-evergreen forests of Assam and eastern Bengal,
swampy mangrove forests of the Ganges Delta, deciduous forest in the Terai,
and thorn forests in the Western Ghats. In various parts of its range it inhabits
or had inhabited additionally partially open grassland and savanna as well as
taiga forests and rocky habitats.Wikipedia:Citation needed

Biology and behaviour

Social and daily activities

<templatestyles src="Multiple_image/styles.css" />

Captive male South Chinese tiger marking his territory

A captive tiger swimming and playing with a piece of wood in a pool

When not subject to human disturbance, the tiger is mainly diurnal. It does not often climb trees but cases have been recorded. It is a strong swimmer and often bathes in ponds, lakes and rivers, thus keeping cool in the heat of the day. Individuals can cross rivers up to 7 km (4.3 mi) wide and can swim up to 29 km (18 mi) in a day. During the 1980s, a tiger named "Genghis" in Ranthambhore National Park was observed frequently hunting prey through deep lake water.

The tiger is a long-ranging species, and individuals disperse over distances of up to 650 km (400 mi) to reach tiger populations in other areas. Adult tigers lead largely solitary lives. They establish and maintain territories but have much wider home ranges within which they roam. Resident adults of either sex generally confine their movements to their home ranges, within which they satisfy their needs and those of their growing cubs. Individuals sharing the same area are aware of each other's movements and activities. The size of the home range mainly depends on prey abundance, geographic area and sex of the individual. In India, home ranges appear to be 50 to 1,000 km^2 (19 to 386 sq mi) while in Manchuria, they range from 500 to 4,000 km^2 (190 to 1,540 sq mi). In Nepal, defended territories are recorded to be 19 to 151 km^2 (7.3 to 58.3 sq mi) for males and 10 to 51 km^2 (3.9 to 19.7 sq mi) for females.

Young female tigers establish their first territories close to their mother's. The overlap between the female and her mother's territory reduces with time. Males, however, migrate further than their female counterparts and set out at a younger age to mark out their own area. A young male acquires territory either by seeking out an area devoid of other male tigers, or by living as a transient in another male's territory until he is older and strong enough to challenge the resident male. Young males seeking to establish themselves thereby comprise the highest mortality rate (30–35% per year) amongst adult tigers.

To identify his territory, the male marks trees by spraying urine and anal gland secretions, as well as marking trails with scat and marking trees or the ground with their claws. Females also use these "scrapes", as well as urine and scat markings. Scent markings of this type allow an individual to pick up information on another's identity, sex and reproductive status. Females in oestrus will signal their availability by scent marking more frequently and increasing their vocalisations.

Figure 8: *A Siberian tiger swimming at Wuppertal Zoo*

Although for the most part avoiding each other, tigers are not always territorial and relationships between individuals can be complex. An adult of either sex will sometimes share its kill with others, even those who may not be related to them. George Schaller observed a male share a kill with two females and four cubs. Unlike male lions, male tigers allow females and cubs to feed on the kill before the male is finished with it; all involved generally seem to behave amicably, in contrast to the competitive behaviour shown by a lion pride. In his book *Tiger*, Stephen Mills describes a social eating event witnessed by Valmik Thapar and Fateh Singh Rathore in Ranthambhore National Park thus:

<templatestyles src="Template:Quote/styles.css"/>

> *A dominant tigress they called Padmini killed a 250 kg (550 lb) male nilgai – a very large antelope. They found her at the kill just after dawn with her three 14-month-old cubs and they watched uninterrupted for the next ten hours. During this period the family was joined by two adult females and one adult male, all offspring from Padmini's previous litters, and by two unrelated tigers, one female the other unidentified. By three o'clock there were no fewer than nine tigers round the kill.*

Occasionally, male tigers participate in raising cubs, usually their own, but this is extremely rare and not always well understood. In May 2015, Amur tigers were photographed by camera traps in the Sikhote-Alin Bioshpere Reserve. The photos show a male Amur tiger pass by, followed by a female and three cubs within the span of about two minutes.[7] In Ranthambore, a male Bengal

Figure 9: *Tigress in Kanha National Park showing flehmen*

tiger raised and defended two orphaned female cubs after their mother had died of illness. The cubs remained under his care, he supplied them with food, protected them from his rival and sister, and apparently also trained them.

Male tigers are generally more intolerant of other males within their territories than females are of other females. Territory disputes are usually solved by displays of intimidation rather than outright aggression. Several such incidents have been observed in which the subordinate tiger yielded defeat by rolling onto its back and showing its belly in a submissive posture. Once dominance has been established, a male may tolerate a subordinate within his range, as long as they do not live in too close quarters. The most aggressive disputes tend to occur between two males when a female is in oestrus, and may rarely result in the death of one of the males.

Facial expressions include the "defense threat", where an individual bares its teeth, flattens its ears and its pupils enlarge. Both males and females show a flehmen response, a characteristic grimace, when sniffing urine markings but flehmen is more often associated with males detecting the markings made by tigresses in oestrus. Like other *Panthera*, tigers roar, particularly in aggressive situations, during the mating season or when making a kill. There are two different roars: the "true" roar is made using the hyoid apparatus and forced through an open mouth as it progressively closes, and the shorter, harsher "coughing" roar is made with the mouth open and teeth exposed. The "true" roar can be heard at up to 3 km (1.9 mi) away and is sometimes emitted three or four times in succession. When tense, tigers will moan, a sound similar to a roar but more subdued and made when the mouth is partially or completely closed. Moaning can be heard 400 m (1,300 ft) away. Chuffing, soft, low-frequency snorting similar to purring in smaller cats, is heard in more friendly situations. Other vocal communications include grunts, woofs, snarls, miaows, hisses and growls.

Hunting and diet

<templatestyles src="Multiple_image/styles.css" />

An adult tiger showing incisors, canines and part of the premolars and molars, while yawning in Franklin Park Zoo

Bengal tiger subduing an Indian boar at Tadoba National Park

In the wild, tigers mostly feed on large and medium-sized animals, preferring ungulates weighing at least 90 kg (200 lb). They typically have little or no deleterious effect on their prey populations. Sambar deer, chital, barasingha, wild boar, gaur, nilgai and both water buffalo and domestic buffalo are the tiger's prey in India. They also prey on other predators, including dogs, leopards, pythons, sloth bears, and crocodiles.

In Siberia, the main prey species are Manchurian wapiti and wild boar (the two species comprising nearly 80% of the prey selected) followed by sika deer, moose, roe deer, and musk deer. Asiatic black bears and Ussuri brown bears may also fall prey to tigers, and they constitute up to 40.7% of the diet of Siberian tigers depending on local conditions and the bear populations. In Sumatra, prey include sambar deer, muntjac, wild boar, Malayan tapir and orangutan. Like many predators, tigers are opportunistic and may eat much smaller prey, such as monkeys, peafowl and other ground-based birds, hares, porcupines, and fish.

Figure 10: *Bengal tiger attacking a sambar in Ranthambore Tiger Reserve*

Tigers generally do not prey on fully grown adult Asian elephants and Indian rhinoceros but incidents have been reported. More often, it is the more vulnerable small calves that are taken. However, occasionally adult rhinoceros, have fallen victims to tigers, as has been documented in at least three separate incidents.[8] Tigers have been reported attacking and killing elephants ridden by humans during tiger hunts in the 19th century.[9] When in close proximity to humans, tigers will also sometimes prey on such domestic livestock as cattle, horses, and donkeys. Old or wounded tigers, unable to catch wild prey, can become man-eaters; this pattern has recurred frequently across India. An exception is in the Sundarbans, where healthy tigers prey upon fishermen and villagers in search of forest produce, humans thereby forming a minor part of the tiger's diet. Although almost exclusively carnivorous, tigers will occasionally eat vegetation for dietary fibre such as fruit of the slow match tree.

Tigers are thought to be mainly nocturnal predators, but in areas where humans are absent, remote-controlled, hidden camera traps recorded them hunting in daylight.[10] They generally hunt alone and ambush their prey as most other cats do, overpowering them from any angle, using their body size and strength to knock the prey off balance. Successful hunts usually require the tiger to almost simultaneously leap onto its quarry, knock it over, and grab the throat or nape with its teeth. Despite their large size, tigers can reach speeds of about 49–65 km/h (30–40 mph) but only in short bursts; consequently, tigers must be close to their prey before they break cover. If the prey catches wind of the tiger's presence before this, the tiger usually abandons the hunt rather than chase prey or battle it head-on. Horizontal leaps of up to 10 m (33 ft) have been

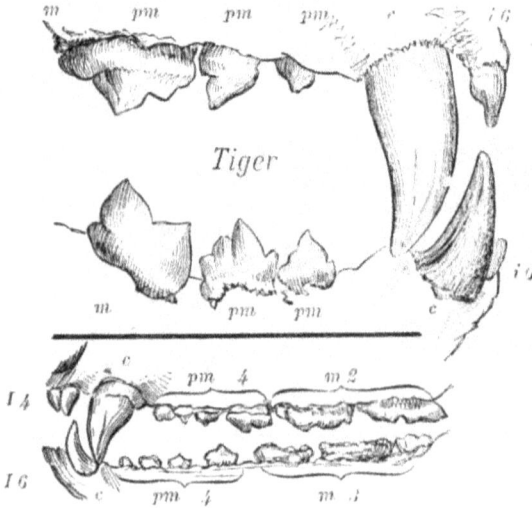

Figure 11: *Tiger dentition (above) and Asian black bear (below).*
The large canines make the killing bite; the carnassials tear flesh.

reported, although leaps of around half this distance are more typical. One in 2 to 20 hunts, including stalking near potential prey, ends in a successful kill.

When hunting larger animals, tigers prefer to bite the throat and use their powerful forelimbs to hold onto the prey, often simultaneously wrestling it to the ground. The tiger remains latched onto the neck until its target dies of strangulation. By this method, gaurs and water buffaloes weighing over a ton have been killed by tigers weighing about a sixth as much.[11] Although they can kill healthy adults, tigers often select the calves or infirm of very large species. Healthy adult prey of this type can be dangerous to tackle, as long, strong horns, legs and tusks are all potentially fatal to the tiger. No other extant land predator routinely takes on prey this large on its own. Whilst hunting sambars, which comprise up to 60% of their prey in India, tigers have reportedly made a passable impersonation of the male sambar's rutting call to attract them.

With smaller prey, such as monkeys and hares, the tiger bites the nape, often breaking the spinal cord, piercing the windpipe, or severing the jugular vein or common carotid artery.[12] Though rarely observed, some tigers have been recorded to kill prey by swiping with their paws, which are powerful enough to smash the skulls of domestic cattle, and break the backs of sloth bears.

After killing their prey, tigers sometimes drag it to conceal it in vegetative cover, usually pulling it by grasping with their mouths at the site of the killing

Figure 12: *Tiger hunted by wild dogs (dholes) as illustrated in Samuel Howett & Edward Orme, Hand Coloured, Aquatint Engravings, 1807*

bite. This, too, can require great physical strength. In one case, after it had killed an adult gaur, a tiger was observed to drag the massive carcass over a distance of 12 m (39 ft). When 13 men simultaneously tried to drag the same carcass later, they were unable to move it. An adult tiger can go for up to two weeks without eating, then gorge on 34 kg (75 lb) of flesh at one time. In captivity, adult tigers are fed 3 to 6 kg (6.6 to 13.2 lb) of meat a day.

Enemies and competitors

Tigers usually prefer to eat prey they have caught themselves, but are not above eating carrion in times of scarcity and may even pirate prey from other large carnivores. Although predators typically avoid one another, if a prey item is under dispute or a serious competitor is encountered, displays of aggression are common. If these are not sufficient, the conflicts may turn violent; tigers may kill competitors as leopards, dholes, striped hyenas, wolves, bears, pythons, and crocodiles on occasion. Tigers may also prey on these competitors.[13,14,15] Attacks on smaller predators, such as badgers, lynxes, and foxes, are almost certainly predatory. Crocodiles, bears, and large packs of dholes may win conflicts against tigers and in some cases even kill them.

The considerably smaller leopard avoids competition from tigers by hunting at different times of the day and hunting different prey.[16] In India's Nagarhole

National Park, most prey selected by leopards were from 30 to 175 kg (66 to 386 lb) against a preference for prey weighing over 176 kg (388 lb) in the tigers. The average prey weight in the two respective big cats in India was 37.6 kg (83 lb) against 91.5 kg (202 lb). With relatively abundant prey, tigers and leopards were seen to successfully coexist without competitive exclusion or interspecies dominance hierarchies that may be more common to the African savanna, where the leopard exists with the lion. Golden jackals may feed on the tiger's kills.[17] Tigers appear to inhabit the deep parts of a forest while smaller predators like leopards and dholes are pushed closer to the fringes.

Reproduction

Wikimedia Commons has media related to *Mating tigers*.

<templatestyles src="Multiple_image/styles.css" />

A Siberian tigress with her cub at the Buffalo Zoo, New York

Two cubs playing with soccer ball at Frankfurt Zoo

Mating can occur all year round, but is more common between November and April. A female is only receptive for three to six days. Mating is frequent and noisy during that time. Gestation ranges from 93 to 112 days, with an average of 103 to 105 days. Litters consist of one or three cubs, rarely as many as six. Cubs weigh from 680 to 1,400 g (1.50 to 3.09 lb) each at birth, and are born blind. Females lactate for five to six months. The female rears them alone, with the birth site and maternal den in a sheltered location such as a thicket, cave or rocky crevice. The father generally takes no part in rearing. Unrelated wandering male tigers often kill cubs to make the female receptive, since the tigress may give birth to another litter within five months if the cubs of the previous litter are lost. The mortality rate of tiger cubs is about 50% in the first two years. Few other predators attack tiger cubs due to the diligence and ferocity of the mother. Apart from humans and other tigers, common causes of cub mortality are starvation, freezing, and accidents.

A dominant cub emerges in most litters, usually a male. This cub is more active than its siblings and takes the lead in their play, eventually leaving its mother and becoming independent earlier. The cubs open their eyes at six to fourteen days old. By eight weeks, the cubs make short ventures outside the den with their mother, although they do not travel with her as she roams her territory until they are older. The cubs are nursed for three to six months. Around the time they are weaned, they start to accompany their mother on territorial walks and they are taught how to hunt. The cubs often become capable (and nearly adult size) hunters at eleven months old. The cubs become independent around eighteen months of age, but it is not until they are around two to two and a half years old that they fully separate from their mother. Females reach sexual maturity at three to four years, whereas males do so at four to five years. The oldest recorded captive tiger lived for 26 years. A wild specimen, having no natural predators, could in theory live to a comparable age.

Generation length of the tiger is about eight years.

Conservation

Tiger population status (2016)

Country	Estimate
Bangladesh	106
Bhutan	103
Cambodia	0
China	>7
India	2,226
Indonesia	371
Laos	2
Malaysia	250
Myanmar	no data
Nepal	198
Russia	433
Thailand	189
Vietnam	<5

Total	3,890

Major threats to the tiger include habitat destruction, habitat fragmentation and poaching for fur and body parts, which have simultaneously greatly reduced tiger populations in the wild. In India, only 11% of the historical tiger habitat remains due to habitat fragmentation.[18] Demand for tiger parts for use in traditional Chinese medicine has also been cited as a major threat to tiger populations. At the start of the 20th century, it was estimated there were over 100,000 tigers in the wild, but the population has dwindled outside of captivity to between 1,500 and 3,500. Some estimates suggest that there are fewer than 2,500 mature breeding individuals, with no subpopulation containing more than 250 mature breeding individuals. The global wild tiger population was estimated by the World Wide Fund for Nature at 3,200 in 2011 and 3,890 in 2015—*Vox* reported that this was the first increase in a century.[19]

India is home to the world's largest population of wild tigers. A 2014 census estimated a population of 2,226, a 30% increase since 2011. In 1973, India's *Project Tiger*, started by Indira Gandhi, established numerous tiger reserves. The project was credited with tripling the number of wild Bengal tigers from some 1,200 in 1973 to over 3,500 in the 1990s, but a 2007 census showed that numbers had dropped back to about 1,400 tigers because of poaching. Following the report, the Indian government pledged $153 million to the initiative, set up measures to combat poaching, promised funds to relocate up to 200,000 villagers in order to reduce human-tiger interactions, and set up eight new tiger reserves. India also reintroduced tigers to the Sariska Tiger Reserve and by 2009 it was claimed that poaching had been effectively countered at Ranthambore National Park.

In the 1940s, the Siberian tiger was on the brink of extinction with only about 40 animals remaining in the wild in Russia. As a result, anti-poaching controls were put in place by the Soviet Union and a network of protected zones (zapovedniks) were instituted, leading to a rise in the population to several hundred. Poaching again became a problem in the 1990s, when the economy of Russia collapsed. The major obstacle in preserving the species is the enormous territory individual tigers require (up to 450 km^2 needed by a single female and more for a single male). Current conservation efforts are led by local governments and NGO's in concert with international organisations, such as the World Wide Fund for Nature and the Wildlife Conservation Society. The competitive exclusion of wolves by tigers has been used by Russian conservationists to convince hunters to tolerate the big cats. Tigers have less impact on ungulate populations than do wolves, and are effective in controlling the latter's numbers. In 2005, there were thought to be about 360 animals in

Figure 13: *Camera trap image of wild Sumatran tiger*

Russia, though these exhibited little genetic diversity. However, in a decade later, the Siberian tiger census was estimated from 480 to 540 individuals.

Having earlier rejected the Western-led environmentalist movement, China changed its stance in the 1980s and became a party to the CITES treaty. By 1993 it had banned the trade in tiger parts, and this diminished the use of tiger bones in traditional Chinese medicine. The Tibetan people's trade in tiger skins has also been a threat to tigers. The pelts were used in clothing, tiger-skin *chuba* being worn as fashion. In 2006 the 14th Dalai Lama was persuaded to take up the issue. Since then there has been a change of attitude, with some Tibetans publicly burning their chubas.

In 1994, the Indonesian Sumatran Tiger Conservation Strategy addressed the potential crisis that tigers faced in Sumatra. The Sumatran Tiger Project (STP) was initiated in June 1995 in and around the Way Kambas National Park in order to ensure the long-term viability of wild Sumatran tigers and to accumulate data on tiger life-history characteristics vital for the management of wild populations.[20] By August 1999, the teams of the STP had evaluated 52 sites of potential tiger habitat in Lampung Province, of which only 15 these were intact enough to contain tigers.[21] In the framework of the STP a community-based conservation programme was initiated to document the tiger-human dimension in the park in order to enable conservation authorities to resolve tiger-human conflicts based on a comprehensive database rather than anecdotes and opinions.[22]

The Wildlife Conservation Society and Panthera Corporation formed the collaboration *Tigers Forever*, with field sites including the world's largest tiger reserve, the 21,756 km² (8,400 sq mi) Hukaung Valley in Myanmar. Other reserves were in the Western Ghats in India, Thailand, Laos, Cambodia, the Russian Far East covering in total about 260,000 km² (100,000 sq mi).

Tigers have been studied in the wild using a variety of techniques. Tiger population have been estimated using plaster casts of their pugmarks, although this method was criticized as being inaccurate. More recent techniques include the use of camera traps and studies of DNA from tiger scat, while radio-collaring has been used to track tigers in the wild. Tiger spray has been found to be just as good, or better, as a source of DNA than scat.

The exact number of wild tigers is unknown, as many estimates are outdated or educated guesses; few estimates are based on reliable scientific censuses. The table shows estimates according to IUCN Red List accounts and range country governments dating from 2009 to April 2016.

Rewilding and reintroduction projects

In 1978, the Indian conservationist Billy Arjan Singh attempted to rewild a tiger in Dudhwa National Park; this was the captive-bred tigress Tara. Soon after the release, numerous people were killed and eaten by a tigress that was subsequently shot. Government officials claimed it was Tara, though Singh disputed this. Further controversy broke out with the discovery that Tara was partly Siberian tiger.[23,24,25]

The organisation Save China's Tigers has attempted to rewild the South China tigers, with a breeding and training programme in a South African reserve known as Laohu Valley Reserve (LVR) and eventually reintroduce them to the wild of China.

A future rewilding project was proposed for Siberian tigers set to be reintroduced to northern Russia's Pleistocene park. The Siberian tigers sent to Iran for a captive breeding project in Tehran are set to be rewilded and reintroduced to the Miankaleh peninsula, to replace the now extinct Caspian tigers.

Figure 14: *A rewilded South China tiger hunting blesbok in South Africa*

Relation with humans

Tiger hunting

The tiger has been one of the big five game animals of Asia. Tiger hunting took place on a large scale in the early 19th and 20th centuries, being a recognised and admired sport by the British in colonial India as well as the maharajas and aristocratic class of the erstwhile princely states of pre-independence India. A single maharaja or English hunter could claim to kill over a hundred tigers in their hunting career. Tiger hunting was done by some hunters on foot; others sat up on *machans* with a goat or buffalo tied out as bait; yet others on elephant-back.[26]

Historically, tigers have been hunted at a large scale so their famous striped skins could be collected. The trade in tiger skins peaked in the 1960s, just before international conservation efforts took effect. By 1977, a tiger skin in an English market was considered to be worth US$4,250.

Traditional medicine

Many people in China and other parts of Asia have a belief that various tiger parts have medicinal properties, including as pain killers and aphrodisiacs. There is no scientific evidence to support these beliefs. The use of tiger parts in pharmaceutical drugs in China is already banned, and the government has made some offences in connection with tiger poaching punishable

Figure 15: *Tiger hunting on elephant-back, India, 1808*

Figure 16: *A hunting party poses with a killed Javan tiger, 1941*

by death.Wikipedia:Avoid weasel words Furthermore, all trade in tiger parts is illegal under the Convention on International Trade in Endangered Species of Wild Fauna and Flora and a domestic trade ban has been in place in China since 1993.

However, the trading of tiger parts in Asia has become a major black market industry and governmental and conservation attempts to stop it have been ineffective to date. Almost all black marketers engaged in the trade are based in China and have either been shipped and sold within in their own country or into Taiwan, South Korea or Japan. The Chinese subspecies was almost completely decimated by killing for commerce due to both the parts and skin trades in the 1950s through the 1970s. Contributing to the illegal trade, there are a number of tiger farms in the country specialising in breeding the cats for profit. It is estimated that between 5,000 and 10,000 captive-bred, semi-tame animals live in these farms today. However, many tigers for traditional medicine black market are wild ones shot or snared by poachers and may be caught anywhere in the tiger's remaining range (from Siberia to India to the Malay Peninsula to Sumatra). In the Asian black market, a tiger penis can be worth the equivalent of around $300 U.S. dollars. In the years of 1990 through 1992, 27 million products with tiger derivatives were found. In July 2014 at an international convention on endangered species in Geneva, Switzerland, a Chinese representative admitted for the first time his government was aware trading in tiger skins was occurring in China.

Man-eating tigers

Wild tigers that have had no prior contact with humans actively avoid interactions with humans. However, tigers cause more human deaths through direct attack than any other wild mammal. Attacks are occasionally provoked, as tigers lash out after being injured while they themselves are hunted. Attacks can be provoked accidentally, as when a human surprises a tiger or inadvertently comes between a mother and her young, or as in a case in rural India when a postman startled a tiger, used to seeing him on foot, by riding a bicycle. Occasionally tigers come to view people as prey. Such attacks are most common in areas where population growth, logging, and farming have put pressure on tiger habitats and reduced their wild prey. Most man-eating tigers are old, missing teeth, and unable to capture their preferred prey. For example, the Champawat Tiger, a tigress found in Nepal and then India, had two broken canines. She was responsible for an estimated 430 human deaths, the most attacks known to be perpetrated by a single wild animal, by the time she was shot in 1907 by Jim Corbett. According to Corbett, tiger attacks on humans are normally in daytime, when people are working outdoors and are not keeping

Figure 17: *Stereographic photograph (1903), captioned "Famous 'man-eater' at Calcutta—devoured 200 men, women and children before capture—India"*

watch. Early writings tend to describe man-eating tigers as cowardly because of their ambush tactics.[27]

Man-eaters have been a particular problem in recent decades in India and Bangladesh, especially in Kumaon, Garhwal and the Sundarbans mangrove swamps of Bengal, where some healthy tigers have hunted humans. Because of rapid habitat loss attributed to climate change, tiger attacks have increased in the Sundarbans. The Sundarbans area had 129 human deaths from tigers from 1969 to 1971. In the 10 years prior to that period, about 100 attacks per year in the Sundarbans, with a high of around 430 in some years of the 1960s. Unusually, in some years in the Sundarbans, more humans are killed by tigers than vice versa. In 1972, India's production of honey and beeswax dropped by 50% when at least 29 people who gathered these materials were devoured. In 1986 in the Sundarbans, since tigers almost always attack from the rear, masks with human faces were worn on the back of the head, on the theory that tigers usually do not attack if seen by their prey. This decreased the number of attacks only temporarily. All other means to prevent attacks, such as providing more prey or using electrified human dummies, worked less well. In 2018 Indian authorities used the perfume *Obsession* by Calvin Klein, containing musk, to attempt to attract and thus trap a wild tiger that had attacked and killed more than a dozen humans.

At least 27 people were killed or seriously injured by captive tigers in the United States from 1998 to 2001.

In some cases, rather than being predatory, tiger attacks on human seem to be territorial in nature. At least in one case, a tigress with cubs killed eight people entering her territory without consuming them at all.

Figure 18: *Tigers made to perform at Ringling Brothers and Barnum and Bailey Circus*

In captivity

In Ancient Roman times, tigers were kept in menageries and amphitheatres to be exhibited, trained and paraded, and were often provoked to fight humans and exotic beasts. Since the 17th century, tigers, being rare and ferocious, were sought after to keep at European castles as symbols of their owners' power. Tigers became central zoo and circus exhibits in the 18th century: a tiger could cost up to 4,000 francs in France (for comparison, a professor of the Beaux-Arts at Lyons earned only 3,000 francs a year), or up to $3,500 in the United States, where a lion cost no more than $1,000.

China (2007) had over 4,000 captive tigers, of which 3,000 were held by about twenty larger facilities, with the rest held by some 200 smaller facilities.[28] The USA (2011) had 2,884 tigers in 468 facilities. Nineteen states have banned private ownership of tigers, fifteen require a license, and sixteen states have no regulation. Genetic ancestry of 105 captive tigers from fourteen countries and regions showed that forty-nine animals belonged distinctly to five subspecies; fifty-two animals had mixed subspecies origins. As such, "many Siberian tigers in zoos today are actually the result of crosses with Bengal tigers."

The Tiger Species Survival Plan has condemned the breeding of white tigers, alleging they are of mixed ancestry and of unknown lineage. The genes responsible for white colouration are represented by 0.001% of the population.

Figure 19: *The Hindu goddess Durga riding a tiger. Guler school, early 18th century*

The disproportionate growth in numbers of white tigers points to inbreeding
among homozygous recessive individuals. This would lead to inbreeding de-
pression and loss of genetic variability.

Cultural depictions

Tigers and their superlative qualities have been a source of fascination for
mankind since ancient times, and they are routinely visible as important cul-
tural and media motifs. They are also considered one of the charismatic
megafauna, and are used as the face of conservation campaigns worldwide.
In a 2004 online poll conducted by cable television channel Animal Planet,
involving more than 50,000 viewers from 73 countries, the tiger was voted the
world's favourite animal with 21% of the vote, narrowly beating the dog.

In myth and legend

In Chinese myth and culture, the tiger is one of the 12 animals of the Chinese
zodiac. In Chinese art, the tiger is depicted as an earth symbol and equal rival of
the Chinese dragon – the two representing matter and spirit respectively. The
Southern Chinese martial art Hung Ga is based on the movements of the tiger

and the crane. In Imperial China, a tiger was the personification of war and often represented the highest army general (or present day defense secretary), while the emperor and empress were represented by a dragon and phoenix, respectively. The White Tiger (Chinese: 白虎 ; pinyin: *Bái Hǔ*) is one of the Four Symbols of the Chinese constellations. It is sometimes called the White Tiger of the West (Chinese: 西方白虎), and it represents the west and the autumn season.

The tiger's tail appears in stories from countries including China and Korea, it being generally inadvisable to grasp a tiger by the tail.

In Buddhism, the tiger is one of the Three Senseless Creatures, symbolising anger, with the monkey representing greed and the deer lovesickness. The Tungusic peoples considered the Siberian tiger a near-deity and often referred to it as "Grandfather" or "Old man". The Udege and Nanai called it "Amba". The Manchu considered the Siberian tiger as "Hu Lin," the king. In Hinduism, the god Shiva wears and sits on tiger skin.[29] The ten-armed warrior goddess Durga rides the tigress (or lioness) Damon into battle. In southern India the god Ayyappan was associated with a tiger.

The weretiger replaces the werewolf in shapeshifting folklore in Asia; in India they were evil sorcerers, while in Indonesia and Malaysia they were somewhat more benign. In the Hindu epic Mahabharata, tigers are fiercer and more ruthless than lions.

In literature, art and film

In William Blake's poem in the *Songs of Experience*, titled "The Tyger," the tiger is a menacing and fearful animal. In Yann Martel's 2001 Man Booker Prize winning novel *Life of Pi*, the protagonist, surviving shipwreck for months in a small boat, somehow avoids being eaten by the other survivor, a large Bengal tiger. The story was adapted in Ang Lee's 2012 feature film of the same name. Jim Corbett's 1944 *Man-Eaters of Kumaon* tells ten true stories of his tiger-hunting exploits in what is now the northern Uttarakhand region of India. The book has sold over four million copies,[30] and has been the basis of both fictional and documentary films. In Rudyard Kipling's 1894 *The Jungle Book*, the tiger, Shere Khan, is the mortal enemy of the human protagonist, Mowgli; the book has formed the basis of both live-action and animated films. Other tiger characters aimed at children tend to be more benign, as for instance Tigger in A. A. Milne's Winnie-the-Pooh and Hobbes of the comic strip *Calvin and Hobbes*, both of whom are represented as simply stuffed animals come to life.

Tiger are also mascots for various sports teams around the world. Tony the Tiger is a famous mascot for Kellogg's breakfast cereal Frosted Flakes. The

Figure 20: *William Blake's first printing of The Tyger, c. 1795*

Esso (Exxon) brand of petrol was advertised from 1969 onwards with the slogan 'put a tiger in your tank', and a tiger mascot; more than 2.5 million synthetic tiger tails were sold to motorists, who tied them to their petrol tank caps.

The tiger appears in heraldry but is distinct from the heraldic beast tyger, a wolflike, snouted creature which has its roots in European Medieval bestiaries.

Political symbolism

The tiger is one of the animals displayed on the Pashupati seal of the Indus Valley Civilisation. The tiger was the emblem of the Chola Dynasty and was depicted on coins, seals and banners.[31] The seals of several Chola copper coins show the tiger, the Pandyan emblem fish and the Chera emblem bow, indicating that the Cholas had achieved political supremacy over the latter two dynasties. Gold coins found in Kavilayadavalli in the Nellore district of Andhra Pradesh have motifs of the tiger, bow and some indistinct marks.[32] The tiger symbol of Chola Empire was later adopted by the Liberation Tigers of Tamil Eelam and the tiger became a symbol of the unrecognised state of Tamil Eelam and Tamil independence movement.[33]

The Bengal tiger is the national animal of India and Bangladesh. The Malaysian tiger is the national animal of Malaysia. The Siberian tiger is the national animal of South Korea. Since the successful economies of South Korea,

Figure 21: *An early silver coin of king Uttama Chola found in Sri Lanka shows the Chola Tiger sitting between the emblems of Pandyan and Chera*

Taiwan, Hong Kong and Singapore were described as the Four Asian Tigers, a tiger economy is a metaphor for a nation in rapid development.

References

A to Z Essays : Essay on Tiger[34]

Bibliography

- John Hampden Porter (1894). "The Tiger"[35]. *Wild beasts; a study of the characters and habits of the elephant, lion, leopard, panther, jaguar, tiger, puma, wolf, and grizzly bear*[36]. pp. 196–256.<templatestyles src="Module:Citation/CS1/styles.css"></templatestyles>
- Sankhala, Kailash (1997). *Indian Tiger*. Roli Books Pvt Limited, India. ISBN 978-81-7437-088-4.<templatestyles src="Module:Citation/CS1/styles.css"></templatestyles>

External links

Wikiquote has quotations related to: *Tigers*

Wikimedia Commonshas media related to:
Panthera tigris(category)

Wikispecieshas information related to *Panthera tigris*

- Species portrait Tiger; IUCN/SSC Cat Specialist Group[37]
- Biodiversity Heritage Library bibliography[38] for *Panthera tigris*
- Tiger Stamps[39]: Tiger images on postage stamps from many different countries
- Year of the tiger[40]. Video collection on occasion of the Year of the Tiger, 2010. BBC.
- Video clips[41]. BBC archive on Wildlife Finder.
- "Is this the last chance to save the tiger?"[42]. 19 November 2010. By Pralad Yonzon. The Kathmandu Post.
- Tale of the Cat[43] at the Wayback Machine (archived 26 February 2010). 1 March 2010. By Andrew Marshall. TIME Magazine
- "India's tiger population increases by 30% in past three years; country now has 2,226 tigers"[44]. 20 January 2015. By Vishwa Mohan. Times of India. Retrieved 17 July 2016.

Appendix

References

[1] Oxford English Dictionary, entry *tiger*

[2] Oxford Dictionary of English Etymology, edited by C.T. Onions, entry *panther*

[3] Oxford Dictionary of English Etymology, edited by C.T. Onions, entry *panther*

[4] Karanth, K. U. (2003). *Tiger ecology and conservation in the Indian subcontinent* https://web.archive.org/web/20121109123727/http://www.nfwf.org/AM/Template.cfm? Section=Home&TEMPLATE=%2FCM%2FContentDisplay.cfm&CONTENTID=8073. *Journal of the Bombay Natural History Society* 100 (2&3) 169–189.

[5] Slaght, J. C., Miquelle, D. G., Nikolaev, I. G., Goodrich, J. M., Smirnov, E., Traylor-Holzer, N. K., Christie, S., Arjanova, T., Smith, J. L. D., Karanth, K. U. (2005). *Chapter 6. Who's king of the beasts? Historical and recent body weights of wild and captive Amur tigers, with comparisons to other subspecies* http://fishowls.com/Slaght%20et%20al%202005.pdf. Pages 25–35 in: Miquelle, D.G., Smirnov, E.N., Goodrich, J.M. (Eds.) *Tigers in Sikhote-Alin Zapovednik: Ecology and Conservation.* PSP, Vladivostok, Russia (in Russian)

[6] Sanderson, E., Forrest, J., Loucks, C., Ginsberg, J., Dinerstein, E., Seidensticker, J., Leimgruber, P., Songer, M., Heydlauff, A., O'Brien, T., Bryja, G., Klenzendorf, S., Wikramanayake, E. (2006). *The Technical Assessment: Setting Priorities for the Conservation and Recovery of Wild Tigers: 2005–2015* https://web.archive.org/web/20120118151415/http://www.worldwildlife.org/species/finder/tigers/WWFBinaryitem9363.pdf. WCS, WWF, Smithsonian, and NFWF-STF, New York and Washington, DC, USA.

[7] Wildlife Conservation Society. (2015). Tiger dad: Rare family portrait of Amur tigers the first-ever to include an adult male https://www.sciencedaily.com/releases/2015/03/150306143548.htm. ScienceDaily, 6 March 2015.

[8] https://www.thehindu.com/news/national/other-states/tiger-kills-adult-rhino-in-dudhwa-tiger-reserve/article4357638.ece .

[9] Frank Leslie's popular monthly, Volume 45, 1879, edited by Frank Leslie, New York: Frank Leslie's Publishing House. 53, 55, & 57 Park Place. p. 411

[10] BBC (2008). *Tiger: Spy In The Jungle* http://www.bbc.co.uk/programmes/b009smrg. John Downer Productions

[11] Sankhala, p. 17

[12] Sankhala, p. 23

[13]

[14] Mills, Gus; Hofer, Heribert (1998). *Hyaenas: status survey and conservation action plan* https://web.archive.org/web/20130506084714/http://data.iucn.org/dbtw-wpd/edocs/1998-013.pdf. IUCN/SSC Hyena Specialist Group.

[15] Miquelle, D.G., Stephens, P.A., Smirnov, E.N., Goodrich, J.M., Zaumyslova, O.Yu. & Myslenkov, A.I. (2005). *Tigers and Wolves in the Russian Far East: Competitive Exclusion, Functional Redundancy and Conservation Implications* https://books.google.com/books?id=ndb0QOvq2LYC&pg=PA179. In *Large Carnivores and the Conservation of Biodiversity.* Ray, J.C., Berger, J., Redford, K.H. & Steneck, R. (eds.) New York: Island Press. pp. 179–207 .

[16] Ecology.info

[17] Sillero-Zubiri, C., Hoffmann, M. and Macdonald, D.W. (eds). 2004. Canids: Foxes, Wolves, Jackals and Dogs. Status Survey and Conservation Action Plan http://www.carnivoreconservation.org/files/actionplans/canids.pdf. IUCN/SSC Canid Specialist Group. Gland, Switzerland and Cambridge, UK.

[18] Dinerstein, E., Loucks, C., Heydlauff, A., Wikramanayake, E., Bryja, G., Forrest, J., Ginsberg, J., Klenzendorf, S., Leimgruber, P., O'Brien, T., Sanderson, E., Seidensticker, J., Songer, M. (2006) *Setting Priorities for the Conservation and Recovery of Wild Tigers: 2005–2015* http://www.panthera.org/content/setting-priorities-conservation-and-recovery-wild-tigers-2005-2015. A User's Guide. 1–50. Washington, D.C., New York, WWF, WCS, Smithsonian, and NFWF-STF.

[19] WWF – Tiger – Overview http://www.worldwildlife.org/species/finder/tigers/index.html. Worldwildlife.org (10 August 2011). Retrieved on 27 September 2011.

[20] Franklin, N., Bastoni, Sriyanto, Siswomartono, D., Manansang, J. and R. Tilson (1999). *Last of the Indonesian tigers: a cause for optimism*, pp. 130–147 in: Seidensticker, J., Christie, S. and Jackson, P. (eds). *Riding the tiger: tiger conservation in human-dominated landscapes*. Cambridge University Press, Cambridge, .

[21] Tilson, R. (1999). *Sumatran Tiger Project Report No. 17 & 18: July – December 1999*. Grant number 1998-0093-059. Indonesian Sumatran Tiger Steering Committee, Jakarta.

[22] Nyhus, P., Sumianto and R. Tilson (1999). *The tiger-human dimension in southeast Sumatra*, pp. 144–145 in: Seidensticker, J., Christie, S. and Jackson, P. (eds). *Riding the tiger: tiger conservation in human-dominated landscapes*. Cambridge University Press, Cambridge, .

[23] Menon, S. (1997). *Tainted Royalty* http://www.india-today.com/itoday/17111997/wild.html . India Today (17 November 1997).

[24] Bagla, P. (19 November 1998). Indian tiger isn't 100 per cent "swadeshi" https://web.archive. org/web/20110204152542/http://www.indianexpress.com/res/web/pIe/ie/daily/19981119/ 32350524.html. The Indian Express.

[25] Singh, R.K. (2000). *Tara: The Cocktail Tigress*. Print World, Allahabad.

[26] *Royal Tiger* (nom-de-plume) in *The Manpoora Tiger – about a Tiger Hunt in Rajpootanah*. (1836) *Bengal Sporting Magazine*, Vol IV. reproduced in *The Treasures of Indian Wildlife*

[27] The Man-Eater of Segur", from *Nine Man-Eaters and One Rogue*, Kenneth Anderson, Allen & Unwin, 1954

[28] Nowell, K., Ling, X. (2007) *Taming the tiger trade: China's markets for wild and captive tiger products since the 1993 domestic trade ban* https://web.archive.org/web/20120117222507/ http://www.worldwildlife.org/species/finder/tigers/WWFBinaryitem15400.pdf. TRAFFIC East Asia, Hong Kong, China.

[29] SIVKISHEN (17 July 2014) *Kingdom of Shiva*, PartridgeIndia, p. 301.

[30] Booth, Martin (1991) *Carpet Sahib; A Life of Jim Corbett*, New York: Oxford University Press, , p. 230.

[31] Hermann Kulke, K Kesavapany, Vijay Sakhuja (2009) *Nagapattinam to Suvarnadwipa: Reflections on the Chola Naval Expeditions to Southeast Asia*, Institute of Southeast Asian Studies, p. 84.

[32] Singh, U. (2008). *A History of Ancient and Early Medieval India: From the Stone Age to the 12th Century* https://books.google.com/books?id=H3lUIIYxWkEC&pg=PAfront. Pearson Education, India.

[33] Daya Somasundaram (11 February 2014) *Scarred Communities: Psychosocial Impact of Man-made and Natural Disasters on Sri Lankan Society*, SAGE Publications India, p. 73.

[34] https://www.atozessays.com/animals/essay-on-wild-animal-tiger/

[35] https://archive.org/stream/wildbeastsstud00port#page/239

[36] https://archive.org/stream/wildbeastsstud00port#page/n0/mode/2up

[37] http://www.catsg.org/index.php?id=124

[38] https://www.biodiversitylibrary.org/name/Panthera_tigris

[39] https://web.archive.org/web/20090605030601/http://www.stampsbook.org/subject/Tiger.html

[40] http://www.bbc.co.uk/nature/collections/p0063wt7

[41] http://www.bbc.co.uk/nature/species/Tiger

[42] https//web.archive.org

[43] https://web.archive.org/web/20100226173448/http://www.time.com/time/magazine/article/0, 9171,1964894-1,00.html

[44] http//timesofindia.indiatimes.com

Article Sources and Contributors

The sources listed for each article provide more detailed licensing information including the copyright status, the copyright owner, and the license conditions.

Tiger *Source:* https://en.wikipedia.org/w/index.php?oldid=865369181 *License:* Creative Commons Attribution-Share Alike 3.0 *Contributors:* 1256wiki, A loose noose, Achat1999, Aditya4wiki, Ankur Bhandari, Apokryltaros, BD2412, BDD, BaldBoris, BhagyaMani, Bharat mags, Brandmeister, BrayLockBoy, Caftaric, Chiswick Chap, Chris the speller, ClueBot NG, CommonsDelinker, Dan100, Davernck, Dhksml1, Dibyendu Ash, DrRC, Elmidae, Esagurton, Fp1998, Frietjes, Gaurav, Gene Wilson, GermanJoe, Grendelkhan, HLHJ, Hanif Al Husaini, Hedwig in Washington, IceBrotherhood, Ira Leviton, Jarble, Jerzy, Jts1882, Kaldari, KylieTastic, LRW UR Editor, Leo1pard, Lerdsuwa, LittleJerry, Loopy30, Magyar25, Maias, Metadat, Meters, Mmkhan.mmk, Nbarth, Nick.mon, Nidasharif, Onel5969, Pannna, Pbrower2a, Piterkeo, Plantdrew, Punetor i Rregullt5, QuartierLatin1968, Quietconcerned8, R'n'B, Regaliceratops, Rjwilmsi, Rodw, Roentgenium111, SHM198, SUM1, Saberrex-Strongheart, Samsara, Shady59, ShakespeareFan00, SilverTiger12, Smithriedel, StephenMikeRodriguez, SuperTah, Tassedethe, Thalassophoneus, Tom.Reding, Tpbradbury, Ubba abba, Volunteer1234, Warrenfrank, Wikiklaas 1

Image Sources, Licenses and Contributors

The sources listed for each image provide more detailed licensing information including the copyright status, the copyright owner, and the license conditions.

License

Index